To drive
on one's own side of the highway
is the first principle in the
etiquette of the road.
1907

# . . FIFTEEN REASONS . .

### WHY

## *An autocar is better than a horse-drawn vehicle.*

~~~~~~~

BECAUSE

1. It wants no stable—the coach-house is enough.
2. It needs no daily grooming, consequently
3. No man need be kept specially to look after it.
4. There is no manure heap to poison the air.
5. It cannot shy, kick, or run away.
6. It has no will of its own to thwart the wishes of its driver and cause disaster.
7. It is more absolutely under control than any horse.
8. It costs nothing to keep, and cannot "eat its head off in the stable."
9. It consumes only when working, and then in exact proportion to the work done.
10. It cannot fall sick and die.
11. It will do more work than any two horses, and
12. Will travel twice as fast as any one.
13. It can be stopped with certainty and safety in half the distance.
14. No cruelty is inflicted by climbing a steep hill with a full load ;
15. Nor can distress be caused by high speed travelling.

# The
# ETIQUETTE
## of
# MOTORING

**Compiled by
Nat Barnes**

*Copper Beech Publishing*

Published in Great Britain by
Copper Beech Publishing Ltd
© Copper Beech Publishing Ltd 1997

ISBN 1 898617 15 5

A CIP catalogue record for this book is available from the
British Library.

Copper Beech Publishing Ltd
P O Box 159 East Grinstead
Sussex England RH19 4FS

# Introduction by Lord Montagu of Beaulieu

*Motor vehicles first appeared legally on British roads on November 14th 1896, and rare as cars were in those days my father bought his first car, a 6 hp Daimler, in 1898. The dust and noise created by early motor-cars caused enormous resentment, particularly as they were owned by a small band of wealthy people whose vehicles frightened horses, cyclists and pedestrians.*

*My father, then the Member of Parliament for the New Forest, quickly became recognised as the spokesman for the new industry. From the start he was most concerned to encourage his fellow motorists to take heed of other road users and do all they could not to cause offence or resentment. He published a series of books called "The Art of Driving a Motor Car", in which he exhorted motorists:*

*"When meeting or overtaking lady cyclists, do not steer too close to them ... Drive slowly when you see a drunken man on the road ... The road is free for all: therefore be courteous and considerate, and ...*
*... ALWAYS DRIVE LIKE A GENTLEMAN."*

*In 1899 my father had the privilege of taking the future King Edward VII for a drive in the New Forest and later for his first trip in a motor car as King.*

*On completing a drive in the New Forest, the Prince of Wales, observing that his lady companions were having difficulty in keeping their hats on, remarked that obviously fashions would have to change with the advent of the car.*

*As the century progressed things came to a head with the Motor Car Bill of 1903 which contained a lot of anti-motorist legislation, and it fell to my father to guide it through the House of Commons. Due to his efforts a compromise was agreed, by which the speed limit could be increased from 12 to 20 mph and number plates on vehicles would be made compulsory.*

*Number plates were introduced on January 1st 1904 and there was no doubt that they not only made it easier for the police to apprehend bad drivers, but also made motorists drive more responsibly.*

*Let my father have the last word: "The whole art of motor-car driving consists in possessing the power of complete control in every sense over yourself and your motor-car at all times. This is the highest ideal to which a motor-car driver can attain.*

*Montagu of Beaulieu*

## THE FIRST-RATE DRIVER

*Quick to observe ... quick to act*

**A**lmost anybody can learn the elementary part of motor driving, but few attain the perfection of competence which implies an acute sympathy with the vehicle being controlled.

**What is required is** a vision quick to observe, a mind quick to notice, hands quick to act, in essence the perfect ear and touch.

**The first-rate driver of a motor-car** anticipates every variation of the mechanism under his control, preventing, rather than waiting to correct its aberrations, foreseeing and avoiding difficulties of traffic rather than extricating himself from them!

The driver should note the hundred and one trifling incidents in the behaviour of the motor-car that go to make up its life and idiosyncrasies.

## CONTROLLING A VEHICLE

*Distances have to be judged
with great exactness ...*

**B**efore even learning to steer a motor-car it is necessary to know how to control any vehicle on the public roads.

**People who make the best drivers** of motor-cars are those who have been accustomed to handle yachts and small boats.

The next best training is that afforded by the ordinary bicycle; it trains the eye to a judgement of distances and to steering on the ordinary public roads. All the same, it must be remembered that the bicycle is a machine steered by balance.

Steering on a bicycle is really a matter of will more than of muscular action. Nevertheless, as the speed of a bicycle is commonly in excess of the ordinary road vehicles its use is a very good introduction to the science and art of motoring.

**Next to the bicycle** the best means of learning to drive a motor-car is probably the horse-drawn trap. In this the driver cannot or ought not to act merely subconsciously as in the case of the bicycle – he must be alert to the conditions surrounding him.

In order to produce a change in the direction or speed of his vehicle the driver must not only experience an impulse in himself, but must communicate it to the animal drawing his carriage!

*The width of a horse-drawn vehicle,*
*being approximately that of a motor-car,*
*provides a valuable education and experience*
*in driving in traffic.*

Distances have to be judged with great exactness, and the driver must know at a glance whether or not there is room for his vehicle to pass.

## LEARNING TO STEER

*The concentration required*
*will possibly prove exhausting ...*

**E**quipped with some experience on the road as an introduction to motoring, the novice will find steering a matter very easily learned. This should be practised, if possible, on an empty road.

The engine having been started, the car should be put on its first speed and an experienced motorist should sit controlling the clutch pedal.

**The novice may then set himself to steer straight** along the road for a given distance.

*At first the tendency will be to turn the wheel too far in either direction, so driving the car along a zigzag course!*

If this lesson is properly learned, straight steering will be much easier at a slightly higher speed; but the attention and concentration required will possibly prove exhausting.

**The new driver should begin** by driving on the higher speed only for a few hundred yards at a time.

**Steering practice should be continued** in a large courtyard or level field. Obstacles, such as boxes and cans, should be variously placed on the ground, some of them being only sufficiently far apart to allow the car to pass between without touching them.

*Drive as if you had no brakes.*
**C S Rolls**

## THE PEDALS

*At the driver's feet ...*

**At the driver's feet will be found** two or three pedals. One of these is for operating the clutch. When it is in the normal upward position the clutch is coupled to the fly-wheel by means of a strong spring. When it is depressed by the driver's foot, the clutch is disengaged and the engine runs free without driving the car.

**Another pedal actuates a brake** which works on a drum on the counter-shaft or differential; in the case of a few cars there is a second pedal brake working on a drum on the second-motion shaft.

**A third pedal is often fixed**, and is called the accelerator pedal; when it is depressed, the governor of the engine is thrown out of action and the power developed by the engine is temporarily increased.

*Pass cattle dead slow.*
*They cross the road for the same reason*
*as a chicken – to get to the other side.*
*They will probably choose the moment*
*of your appearance!*

## STARTING THE CAR

*The novice may be ready to make his first essay
in actually driving ...*

**O**nce the novice driver can understand the means of control provided on the standard petrol car, he may be ready to make his first essay in actually driving.

**The first thing to be done** is to see that the respective tanks are filled with water, petrol and lubricating oil.

The driver should now turn on the tap which admits petrol from the tank to the carburettor and switch on whichever of the accumulators he intends to use.

**He should see that the side brake is on** and the clutch disengaged, an additional precaution being adopted in placing the change-speed lever in its middle or neutral position, when none of the gear wheels are in mesh.

**The throttle should then be opened** slightly and the ignition retarded by the placing of the ignition lever in its most backward position.

*The placing of the ignition lever is necessary in order to prevent a back-fire of the engine in starting it and the possible dislocation of the motorist's arm or wrist.*

**To proceed to start his engine** he must stand in front of and facing the car with the starting handle on his right hand.

## AVOIDING INJURY

*Avoid injury if a back-fire occurs ...*

**Placing his left hand** on the curved projecting spring of the car, the driver stoops down and grasps the starting handle with the four fingers of his right hand, but not with the thumb - that is to say, the four fingers should be hooked underneath the handle, and thumb lying loosely along it, and not grasping it as instinct would suggest!

**If the engine is a perfect one**, one pull will be enough to start it, but more likely it will need several rapid turns of the handle.

In making these turns the motorist - if he wishes to avoid the bogey of petrol engines, the back-fire - will hold his hand in the way described and will exert force only in pulling up the handle and not in pushing it down. In this way, even if a back-fire occurs, no injury can be inflicted on the arm or wrist.

# RULES FOR THE ROAD

### *You will have no idea of the horrors ...*

**A**bove all, **have mercy** upon timid women, dogs and little children.

If you have no imagination you will have no idea of the horrors of apprehension suffered by many a woman alone in a pony trap who sees your approach and does not know whether you mean to stop or not. If she makes a sign, hold up your hand to show that you have seen it and go past her (it may not be necessary to stop) as quietly as possible.

**The only thing you need have little mercy on is the unattended horse** dozing in the empty village street. Frighten him, if you like, and chivy him far away from the place of inattention; he is a scourge and a danger; but he will take good care not to hurt himself. And people who have to pay for many sets of broken harness will soon learn not to leave their horses unattended.

**If you are threatened by a dog**, go slowly; he may be a senseless, ill-conditioned, barking cur, but he has a right to his life; and besides, you may be seriously hurt yourself if you run over him. But even upon the little dog have some mercy.

**And as for children**, remember that their minds work in ways that we know not, that our dull senses are no guide to their actions, and that if it seems good to them to play at 'last across,' you had better go very gingerly in their neighbourhood.

In a little while a new generation of children will grow up wary of motor-cars, and trained, poor mites, in the taking of cover; but in the meantime remember that the bit of village street through which you flash on your hundred-mile journey is their life, and contains for them all the sunshine, all the dangers, all the pleasures and toils of life.

## SERVANTS

*A chauffeur should be
a thoroughly capable man ...*

**W**here an owner will drive his own car and supervise its condition he need not employ a skilled motor-man as a rule, as very often an intelligent man-servant or boy can be trained to do the rough work of clearing up.

**A warning** - if a car is to be placed entirely in the charge of a chauffeur, he should be a thoroughly capable man, or if an old servant be selected, the employer should see that he gets the proper tuition before taking over the charge of the car.

*"Heard the news? ... There's nothing else being talked about all along the river bank. Toad went up to Town ... and he has ordered a large and very expensive motor-car."*

**The Wind in the Willows**
**Kenneth Grahame**
**1908**

## THE MOTOR HOOLIGAN

*Remember ... you did not always*
*own a motor-car ...*

**T**here are those in whom mere thought-**lessness** and the intoxication that springs from the control of power and speed has bred the motor hooligan!

Remember, you were once perhaps capable of enjoying a quiet walk on a country road and that you did not always own a motor-car.

**Remember that if you whoop through** a village some Sunday morning in the summertime and meet a crowd of decent villagers going to church, the clouds of dust that you raise may spoil their Sunday clothes, fill their mouths with grit and their hearts with bitterness!

**Horn at approaching carts of the heavy order.**
**There may be a small boy**
**hanging on behind!**

# CARE OF YOUR MOTOR-CAR

### *The ideal motor-house should be substantially built ...*

**I**f a motor-house is to be specially constructed it may either be built of brick or stone, or a very efficient (though less sightly) building may be constructed of corrugated iron and wood.

The ideal motor-house should be substantially built, with a deeply pitched roof containing large skylights. In the middle of the house a motor-pit should be sunk, about 5 feet in depth by 6 feet in length and about 3½ feet in width.

**Outside the motor-house** should be a well-drained pavement for the washing of cars.

Petrol and paraffin oil should be kept in a separate building; the roughest little cabin will do so long as it is thoroughly ventilated. These stores should never be kept in any building adjoining either the motor-house, stables or the living rooms of the servants.

**Sir David Salomons,** whose motor-houses at Broomhill, Tunbridge Wells, are probably the most completely equipped in this country, has devised a special house for the storage of petrol, built of bricks with slight gaps in between so as to allow a free current of air to pass through them.

**If the motor-house is properly warmed** there will be no need for waterproof covers for the car, but it should always be covered with a light dust cover except in very damp weather, when it is better to use no cover at all.

*If the car is to be in the motor-house for several days at a time, it is always well for the sake of the tyres to jack all four wheels up off the floor.*

## ACCESSORIES AND FITTINGS

*It is not advisable for the ordinary motorist
to have a speed recorder ...*

**T**here is no end to the number of fittings
which the enthusiast may have on his dashboard -
most of them very costly and of doubtful utility!

**A good carriage clock** is a necessity and a
gradometer, for measuring the gradients over which
the car is travelling, is a rather interesting accessory
to a touring car.

**Speed recorders or 'speedometers'** are now
made which are supposedly accurate in recording in
miles per hour the rate at which the car is travelling;
but it is doubtful whether they give much pleasure
to the average owner of a car. On the whole, it is not
advisable for the ordinary motorist to have a speed
recorder.

**You may easily spend £30 on a set of lamps** and then in six months time it will be quite easy to spend another £30 on lamps of a newer pattern. But this is unnecessary.

The blinding search lights used on some cars are both disagreeable and dangerous. For ordinary starlight or moonlit nights two good paraffin lamps are all that is necessary.

## CLOTHES FOR MOTORING

*Goggles are, unhappily, almost a necessity ...*

For travelling in all but the warmest weather, garments should be lined with some substance which is impervious to wind, such as chamois leather.

Goggles are, unhappily, almost a necessity, when travelling at any but the lowest speeds; and unlovely as they are to look upon, it is better to be able to keep one's eyes open to see what is going on, even at the cost of temporary disfigurement, than to screw them up and see nothing.

The clouds of gnats and flies that hang in summer just at the elevation at which one's head passes when driving in a motor-car are both unpleasant and dangerous - unpleasant if they get into your mouth and dangerous if they get into your eyes!

## CLOTHES
## FOR THE WOMAN MOTORIST

*Suitable clothing for all the year round ...*

There are two things to be considered; how a woman can keep herself warm in winter and not be suffocated by the dust in summer without making herself very unattractive.

**A warm gown should be adopted**, made of a material that will not catch the dust, and it is also important to wear warm clothing under the gown; for unless such jerseys and bodices are worn, the wind penetrates and it is quite impossible to avoid feeling chilled during a long day.

For ladies, costumes, coats and skirts can be made of thin glove kid, or suede – but these are luxuries and cost from 25 – 30 guineas each. A coat lined with fur or chamois leather is the most successful.

**As to head-gear**, the round cap or close-fitting turban of fur are the most comfortable and suitable, though with the glass screen up it is possible to wear an ordinary hat, with a veil round it.

**It is a good plan to have caps made** to match your costumes. When fixing the cap, pin it securely, and over it put a crêpe-de-chine veil of length a-plenty. These can be obtained from most of the leading drapers, and it is quite a simple matter to make them yourself with a length of crêpe or washing silk. Before tying the veil, twist the ends.

This prevents the knot working loose and is very necessary, as the veil, in addition to protecting the hair, helps to keep the hat securely in place.

THE MOTOR BURBERRY

## MOTOR-CARS AND HEALTH

*The great benefit derived from the invigorating
and refreshing effect of driving ...*

**Ladies with defective nerve power** have
derived great benefit from the invigorating and
refreshing effect caused by driving in an automobile.
Furthermore, the action of the air on the face and the
continual inspiration of fresh air, tend to promote
sleep; daily exercise in a motor-car is an aid towards
the prevention of insomnia.

**It is difficult to exaggerate** the necessity for
those who live in the densely populated parts of cities
to take every possible opportunity of breathing the
purer air of the country.

**The air in towns** is impregnated with carbon
and in dry weather, loaded with dust, a great part of
which is composed of dried and pulverised horse
manure. These impurities are practically absent from
the air of the country.

**Men who are occupied long and closely with brain-work** state that the automobile has filled a great want in their lives. They have found themselves too exhausted to be able to take a long bicycle ride into the country; while railway travelling increases their sense of fatigue.

**The effort to catch a train at a definite time** is in itself irritating and wearing to an over-worked system. A drive behind a horse scarcely amounts to a recreation after the worry of work.

**In the automobile**, however, he finds ample sources of interest, amounting to a gentle, healthy excitement with complete absence of fatigue.

*A few words of caution ...*
*The vigorous man who has been used to taking*
*exercise on horseback, on his bicycle or on his legs*
*must beware lest the fascination of motoring lead*
*him to give up his physical exercise.*

*Unless he systematically maintains habits of*
*muscular exertion he may find that he is putting*
*on flesh, becoming flabby and generally losing*
*condition.*

*Never take a sharp corner at full speed.*
*A walking pace would be much better.*

# THE DUST NUISANCE

*Others have the right to use the road ... without being smothered in dust ...*

**Dust is the bête noire of motorists,** but at the same time, its effects are often exaggerated.

The trouble is caused by the suction behind the car, which draws dust after it. Consequently, if there is a low back seat to the car the dust streams in, and not only smothers the rear passengers but even reaches those in the front seat. Hoods and 'dust screens' are now available.

**The chief grievance that road users have** against motorists is the selfishness they display in the matter of raising dust. A large proportion of motorists are absolutely selfish and deserve the appellation of cads and hooligans and 'road hogs' which are freely given to them.

**In order to satisfy their desire for a faster pace**, they appear to enjoy raising a dust ten times worse than that raised by a coach and four.

It never appears to enter the heads of these persons that others have a right to use the high road as well as themselves, without being smothered with dust; and that if the road be dusty, it is their duty to look back, and if they see that they are raising an amount of dust greater than that of a carriage and pair, to moderate their pace forthwith.

*Motorists cannot expect authorities to remake roads to suit their convenience.*

Doubtless much will be done to make roads less dusty; it seems more probable that the mere raising of unusual dust will ere long be held to be an offence both as a nuisance to the public, and as tending to obscure the view of the number plate.

## TIPPING

*Motor-car owners are not necessarily
millionaires ...*

**I**f there is one thing more than another
which the motor-car has revived and intensified it is
the habit and practice of tipping.

**The garage tip is a necessary tip**, whether the
garage be a public one or at the house of a friend; also,
if a friend lends you a car for a drive - or your friend's
chauffeur drives you to the railway station  in very
bad weather - it would be impolite not to tip.

As the motor-car comes more into general use,
the chauffeur, attendants and servants are beginning
to understand that their owners are not necessarily
millionaires, and they can no longer expect a handful
of money from every motorist.

## TOURING

### *To fail to climb a hill ...*

**The question as to what roads** are most reliable for motoring depends, of course, much on the car. With a low powered car, say 6 or 8 hp or less, it will not usually be advisable to plan a long tour without careful consideration of the hills, and particularly the gradients that have to be met.

**It is always annoying** and may be dangerous to fail to climb a hill owing to want of power of the engine or skill of manipulation!

*'Mile for mile, the car is less expensive than
the horse-drawn carriage, besides
being faster and considerably
more comfortable!' 1903*

**Contributed to Autocar by a country doctor who had substituted a motor car for his single horse and trap:**

| Horse Expenses per year | £ | s | d |
|---|---|---|---|
| Horse expenses (15s per week includes food hay and straw) | 40 | 0 | 0 |
| Shoeing | 4 | 0 | 0 |
| Veterinary account | 2 | 0 | 0 |
| Harness repairs | 1 | 10 | 0 |
| Carriage repairs | 12 | 10 | 0 |
| Coachman 26s per week | 67 | 0 | 0 |
| Livery/Boots/Whips/Sponges | 3 | 0 | 0 |
| **TOTAL** | **£130** | **0** | **0** |

| Motor-Car Expenses per year | £ | s | d |
|---|---|---|---|
| Tyres | 20 | 0 | 0 |
| Petrol 100 miles a week at 1s per gallon for 25 miles | 10 | 10 | 0 |
| Repairs | 12 | 10 | 0 |
| Youth at 15s per week | 40 | 0 | 0 |
| Sponges, leather etc | 1 | 0 | 0 |
| **TOTAL** | **£84** | **0** | **0** |

## MOTORING MATTERS

### *Pioneer motorists ...*

Among the pioneer motorists in Great Britain were Lord Montagu of Beaulieu, The Hon C S Rolls, Sir David Salomons, J H Knight, Col. Compton, TRB Elliot, J A Koosen, Frank Butler, Sir John MacDonald, R J Mecredy, A J Wilson, Henry Sturney, Stanley Spooner, S F Edge, and Charles Jarrott.

Of all the pioneers, perhaps most credit goes to Lord Montagu who, as the Hon John Scott Montagu first interested the future King Edward VII (then Prince of Wales) in this new pastime. His great enthusiasm and influence cleared the way for the motor-car through British prejudice and conservatism.

## MOTORING MATTERS

### *Rudyard Kipling ...*

Rudyard Kipling was one of the early motorists whom many called maniacs and with good reason.

Kipling's interest in motoring began shortly before the turn of the century. And it is fair to say it would have begun earlier still if he had been living in England instead of America in 1895. Then, on his return to England in 1899 he was visited by Alfred Harmsworth of the Daily Mail in his new motor-car.

Kipling's first 'Very-Own' motor was an American Locomobile that ran on a mixture of petrol, steam and water. His next car was a 2-cylinder, 10hp Lanchester, delivered to Kipling's door in Sussex by Frederick Lanchester himself. Between 1906 and 1910 though, a Daimler occupied the converted coachhouse at Bateman's.

## MOTORING MATTERS

Then, in 1910 came a chance meeting with Lord Montagu and 'an enormous 6 cyl Rolls Royce'.

Kipling purchased his first Rolls Royce, a limousine landaulet costing £800, in 1911 and nicknamed it The Green Goblin.

The Kiplings took annual motoring holidays and Kipling kept journals of his Motor Tours.

The many Rolls Royce motor-cars owned by Rudyard Kipling were all green and perhaps most astonishing of all is the fact that Kipling never drove himself, but always used a chauffeur!

## MOTORING MATTERS

### *The 'Red Flag' Law ...*

When motor cars were first imported to Britain, the 'Red Flag' law (Locomotives Act of 1865) was still in force, and the cars were treated as traction engines – and as such had to be driven at a speed limit of four miles an hour, and be preceded by a man on foot carrying a red flag!

### *Exceeding the speed limit ...*

Walter Arnold was charged on 28th January 1896 at Tonbridge with exceeding the 2mph speed limit at Paddock Wood. It was estimated that he was doing 8mph when stopped by a policeman on a bicycle after a five mile chase. He was fined one shilling.

## MOTORING MATTERS

### *The Act repealed ...*

Evelyn Ellis decided openly to challenge the Red Flag Act. In November 1896 he broke the law by driving his car to London without a man walking in front with a red flag. The following morning, he and 50 other car owners gathered their vehicles on the Thames Embankment and before a crowd of more than 5000 people, drove to Brighton.

On 14th November 1896 the Act was repealed and motors were allowed to drive on the highway at a speed not exceeding 12mph.

In 1903 British motorists received another charter which, by increasing the speed limit from 12 to 20 mph, enabled more powerful cars to be used.

## MOTORING MATTERS

### *The first motor show ...*

The World's first exhibition of motor vehicles was organised by Sir David Salomons at the Agricultural Showground, Tunbridge Wells in Kent on 15th October 1895, just six months before the first motor show in the United States of America.

## Tunbridge Wells

# AGRICULTURAL SHOW GROUND.

# HORSELESS

# CARRIAGE

# TRIALS,

## On Tuesday, Oct. 15th

### SIR DAVID SALOMONS

WILL EXHIBIT HIS

# PETROLEUM CARRIAGE

### And a few other Horseless Carriages,

By the kindness of Friends, at the above Show Ground, which has been lent him for the occasion.

## The Carriages will enter the Ring at 3.0 p.m.

A Limited number of Invitation Tickets have been issued, and the Public will be admitted on the Payment of 1s. each.

The Money so collected will be employed for Prizes for Self-Propelled Carriages for Agricultural, Trade and Private Purposes at the next Agricultural Show, the Expenses of the Exhibition being defrayed by the Exhibitor.

Printed by the "Courier" Company, Grove Hill Road, Tunbridge Wells.

## MOTORING MATTERS

*Motoring clubs ...*

In an attempt to form an independent body to champion the cause of motorists, Frederick Richard Simms started the 'Automobile Club of Great Britain' in July 1897.

Ten years later it became the Royal Automobile Club with the patronage of King Edward VII.

At a time when people asked to touch the King's Daimler as though it were a talisman, the RAC's new royal title gave it an aura of prestige.

The RAC was also involved with the creation of the famous Brooklands track which opened in Weybridge, Surrey in 1907.

The Ladies Automobile Club of Great Britain & Ireland was established in 1903. Its headquarters were situated at Claridge's Hotel.

*'By this time next year ... the motor car will be everywhere seen.'*
**Vanity Fair 1899.**

## Acknowledgements

The compiler and publishers would like to thank the following:

Lord Montagu of Beaulieu
National Motoring Museum Library, Beaulieu
Photograph of Edward VII and John Scott Montagu used with permission.
The David Salomons Society
Thanks to Random House for permission to quote from The Complete
Motorist, Filson Young
Extracts from 'The Woman and The Car' by Dorothy Levitt
by kind permission of the publishers, Bodley Head
Extract from 'The Wind in the Willows' by Kenneth Grahame
copyright The University Chest, Oxford, reproduced by
permission of Curtis Brown, London
The Museum Royal Tunbridge Wells
RAC
The National Trust Bateman's

Motor clothes reproduced by kind permission of Burberrys
Quotations from Autocar used by kind permission
Other pictures from private collections

Titles used in the research of this book include:
The Complete Motorist, Filson Young
The Art of Driving a Motor Car Lord Montagu
The Woman and The Car Dorothy Levitt
Kipling The Motoring Man, Meryl Macdonald
The Motoring Century,
The Story of the Royal Automobile Club, Piers Brendon

## THE ETIQUETTE COLLECTION
### *Collect the set!*

### ETIQUETTE FOR COFFEE LOVERS
Fresh coffee - the best welcome in the world!
Enjoy the story of coffee drinking,
coffee etiquette and recipes.

### ETIQUETTE FOR CHOCOLATE LOVERS
Temptation through the years.
A special treat for all Chocolate Lovers.

### THE ETIQUETTE OF NAMING THE BABY
A good name keeps its lustre in the dark.
Old English Proverb

### THE ETIQUETTE OF ENGLISH PUDDINGS
Traditional recipes for good old-fashioned
puddings - together with etiquette notes for serving.

### ETIQUETTE FOR GENTLEMEN
*"If you have occasion to use your handkerchief
do so as noiselessly as possible."*

A Copper Beech Book makes the perfect gift. See also our books
about parlour games, servants, graphology and social secrets.

## THE ETIQUETTE COLLECTION
### *Collect the set!*

### THE ETIQUETTE OF AN ENGLISH TEA
How to serve a perfect English afternoon tea;
traditions, superstitions, recipes and how to read your
fortune in the tea-leaves afterwards.

### THE ETIQUETTE OF POLITENESS
Good sense and good manners.
How to be polite and well-bred at all times.

### THE ETIQUETTE OF DRESS
Fashion tips from bygone days.

### THE ETIQUETTE OF LOVE AND COURTSHIP
A guide for romantics.
Flirting, temptation, first impressions:
essential advice for lovers.

For your free catalogue containing these and other Copper Beech
Gift Books, write to:

Copper Beech Publishing Ltd
P O Box 159 East Grinstead Sussex England RH19 4FS